The Merchant of Venice

About Wise & Wide

- A systematic 6-level English reading program based on Lexile® measures
- Diverse and interesting topics chosen from the elementary curriculums of Korea and English speaking western countries
- Well-written books in various forms including fiction stories, descriptive texts, and classics retold
- The informative but original fiction stories grab your interest, leading to the easy and clear understanding of the educational content.
- Improve thinking skills with solid after-reading activities at all levels of the series.

Wise & Wide is a 6-level English reading program that consists of 60 books and each level is systematically divided by Lexile® measures. The Lexile® Framework for Reading is the most popular reading measuring system in American formal education curriculums and many English programs. Over 20 out of 50 states in the U.S. mark Lexile® measures directly on students' final report cards and over 300 well-known publishers adopt and use Lexile® measures.

Experience many kinds of readings written by professional writers from the U.S. and England. They used interesting topics that were carefully chosen after analyzing elementary curriculums from around the world including Korea, the U.S., England, and Australia among many others. Comprehensive after-reading activities including graphic organizers, speaking tasks, and After-reading Tests are ready for you.

Levels in the series and their corresponding Lexile® measures

Level	Lexile® measures	U.S. Grade
Level 1	Below 200L	Pre K - K
Level 2	190L - 400L	Lower Grade 1
Level 3	350L - 530L	Upper Grade 1
Level 4	420L - 650L	Grade 2
Level 5	520L - 940L	Grade 3 - 4
Level 6	830L - 1070L	Grade 5 - 6

* Smart Readers: Wise & Wide level 1 is applicable to the preschool level in the U.S.

* The source of the relationship between Lexile® measures and U.S. school grades: CCSS(Common Core State Standards) FOR ENGLISH LANGUAGE ARTS, APPENDIX A (2012, which is used by 45 states in the U.S.)

Topic List

	Level 1	Level 2	Level 3	Level 4	Level 5	Level 6
Book 1	Science>Biology: The hibernation of animals Story	Science>Biology: Living and nonliving things Story	Science>Biology> Animals & the Environment: Sea otters Story	Environment> Living with nature: The diver & the persimmon tree Story	Science>Biology> Animal: Amazing animals of the Amazon Story	Science>Biology: Germs, transmitted diseases Story
Book 2	Literature> World classics: Aesop's fables Story	Literature> Traditional fairy tale: Old tales about stones Story	Social Studies> Economy: To run a business to make and save money Story	Science>Biology> Plants: Photosynthesis Story	Science>Earth science: Earth's layers, earthquakes, volcanoes, and earth's atmosphere Report	Mathematics> Sequence: The golden ratio & the Fibonacci sequence Story
Book 3	Science>Physics: How shadows are formed Story	Literature> World classics: Peter Pan Story	Science>Scientific technology: Nanobots Story	Literature>Myths: World's creation stories Story	Literature> Legend: The story of King Arthur Story	Literature>Myths: Constellation myths Story
Book 4	Literature> Traditional literature: The Talmud Story	Science>Biology> Animal: Polar bears Story	Science>Biology> Animal: Mountain gorillas Story	Social Studies> Cultural anthropology: Amazing ancient cultures of the world Story	Science> Earth science: Clouds and weather Story	Literature> Human & animals: The friendship between a girl and a horse Story
Book 5	Social Studies> Ethics: Rules in daily life Story	Science>Biology: The five senses Report	Social Studies> Cultural anthropology: Astonishing festivals Report	Art>Music: Stories from two operas Story	Social Studies> World culture & history: The Renaissance Story	Sports> Board sports: Surfing & snowboarding Story
Book 6	Social Studies> World geography & travel: Tourist attractions around the world Story	Science>Biology> Animal: Dinosaurs Story	Science> Astronomy: The solar system Story	Social Studies> People: Three great people who overcame hardships Story	Science>Scientific technology: The wonderful world of robots Report	Art>Music: Composers of the Romantic Era Report
Book 7	Science> Space science: The life of astronauts Report	Social Studies> Cultural anthropology: Mythological monsters from around the world Report	Mathematics> Elementary mathematics: Numbers, measurement, shapes and data Report	Science & Social Studies> Technology & culture: Inventions from around the world Report	Art>Works of art: Famous paintings Report	Social Studies> Human & animals: Animals in action for human Report
Book 8	Social Studies> Cultural anthropology: Various living cultures of the world Story	Art>Music: Instruments in the orchestra Story	Social Studies> Life safety: Learning and using outdoor survival skills Story	Social Studies> History: The California Gold Rush Report	Social Studies & Science> Psychology: Psychology in everyday life Story	Literature> World classics: The Merchant of Venice Story
Book 9	Social Studies> Jobs: Interviews about jobs Report	Science>Scientific technology: Developments in technology in different times Story	Social Studies> Politics>Election: Running for 3rd grade class president Story	Literature> World classics: Stories of Sherlock Holmes Story	Literature> World classics: Adrift in the Pacific Story	
Book 10		Sports>Winter sports: Various aspects of some Winter Olympic sports Report		Sports> Ball games: Various aspects of popular ball games Report		

* 10 books in each level will be published.

How to Use This Book

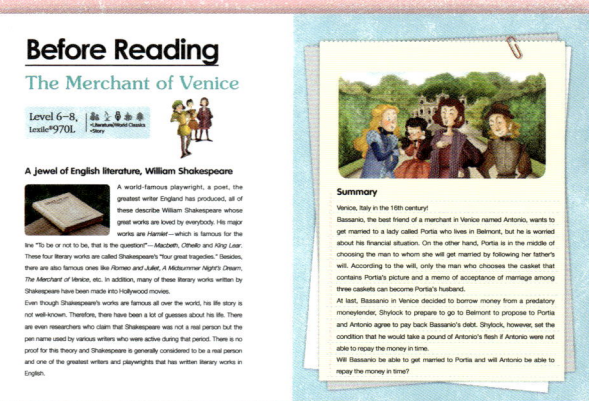

•Before Reading

You can easily find the topic and what kind of story you are about to read.

•The text

All the stories were written by professional writers from the U.S. and England, so you will read authentic and appropriate English sentences and expressions in every book in the series.

•Pop Quiz

Check out right away if you understand what you have just read by solving a pop quiz that checks your comprehension.

•Key Words

The key words and expressions on each page are listed for you to easily study them.

•Aha! Tips

Download free Korean explanations at *www.ihappyhouse.co.kr* for all of the sentences marked with "Aha!". These explain cultural, scientific, and economic knowledge or they deal with aspects of English such as grammatical structures or idiomatic expressions. There are lots of "Aha! Tips" to help you understand the text.

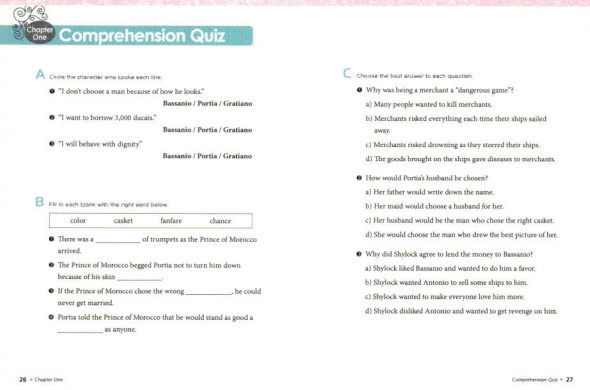

•Comprehension Quiz

After reading one chapter, solve various questions to find out if you fully understand the content.

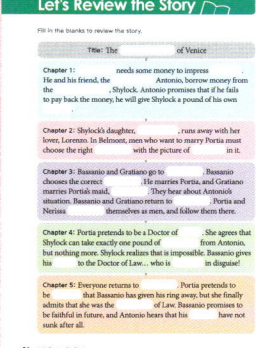 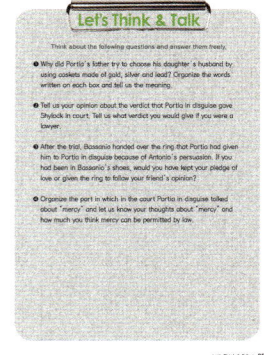

•Let's Review the Story /
•Let's Think & Talk

Fill in the blanks in the organizer to summarize the whole story. Express your own thinking and feelings about the story by answering the questions. You can build up logic and reasoning skills for your essay examinations in the future.

Appendix

Audio CD

In the CD audio book form, the texts are read vividly by American professional voice actors. (MP3 files downloaded for free)

After-reading Test

Solve an additionally provided After-reading Test for each book.

The Korean translation, Answer Keys, a Word Quiz, a Word List, and Aha! Tips for each book

You can download them for free at *www.ihappyhouse.co.kr* or *www.darakwon.co.kr*

Before Reading

The Merchant of Venice

Level 6–8,
Lexile®970L

•Literature)World Classics
•Story

A jewel of English literature, William Shakespeare

A world-famous playwright, a poet, the greatest writer England has produced, all of these describe William Shakespeare whose great works are loved by everybody. His major works are *Hamlet*—which is famous for the line "To be or not to be, that is the question!"—*Macbeth*, *Othello* and *King Lear*. These four literary works are called Shakespeare's "four great tragedies." Besides, there are also famous ones like *Romeo and Juliet*, *A Midsummer Night's Dream*, *The Merchant of Venice*, etc. In addition, many of these literary works written by Shakespeare have been made into Hollywood movies.

Even though Shakespeare's works are famous all over the world, his life story is not well-known. Therefore, there have been a lot of guesses about his life. There are even researchers who claim that Shakespeare was not a real person but the pen name used by various writers who were active during that period. There is no proof for this theory and Shakespeare is generally considered to be a real person and one of the greatest writers and playwrights that has written literary works in English.

Summary

Venice, Italy in the 16th century!

Bassanio, the best friend of a merchant in Venice named Antonio, wants to get married to a lady called Portia who lives in Belmont, but he is worried about his financial situation. On the other hand, Portia is in the middle of choosing the man to whom she will get married by following her father's will. According to the will, only the man who chooses the casket that contains Portia's picture and a memo of acceptance of marriage among three caskets can become Portia's husband.

At last, Bassanio in Venice decided to borrow money from a predatory moneylender, Shylock to prepare to go to Belmont to propose to Portia and Antonio agree to pay back Bassanio's debt. Shylock, however, set the condition that he would take a pound of Antonio's flesh if Antonio were not able to repay the money in time.

Will Bassanio be able to get married to Portia and will Antonio be able to repay the money in time?

Contents

The Merchant of Venice

The Merchant of Venice

A Generous Friend

In the 16th century, Europe was full of merchants — men who made their money by buying and selling goods. In those days, the only way to send goods to the people who wanted to buy them was by ship, and the seas were often stormy. It was a dangerous game for those who lived this way, risking everything each time their ships sailed away.

One such merchant, Antonio, lived in Venice, Italy. He was worried one day, thinking about the fate of his ships. Every time the breeze cooled his soup, he thought about the wind wrecking his ships. Every time he went to church and saw the stone from which it was built, he thought about his ships running aground on vicious rocks. His face was solemn and his heart was weighed down by his worries, making his friends concerned about him.

KEY WORDS

- generous
- be full of
- merchant
- make money (make-made-made)
- goods
- in those days
- by ship
- stormy
- game
- risk

- sail
- fate
- breeze
- cool
- wreck
- run aground on (run-ran-run)
- vicious
- solemn
- weigh down
- concerned

A group of young men arrived to join Antonio as he stood in the street, including Antonio's best friend, Bassanio, and two others called Lorenzo and Gratiano. Gratiano loved to mess around and play the fool; his greatest ambition was to grow old laughing, and his friends loved him for it.

"Lots of men are called wise because they say nothing," he said, nodding towards Antonio, who was silent.

"Then I must be the wisest man of all," laughed Lorenzo, "since Gratiano never lets me speak!"

"Gratiano, you do talk a load of rubbish," said Bassanio affectionately, patting his friend on the back.

Antonio spoke up at last, asking Bassanio about the woman whose heart he wanted to win.

"In Belmont there is a rich, beautiful woman called Portia," said Bassanio. "Lots of men want to marry her, but how can I hope to win her heart if I have no fine gifts to offer her? You know that I owe a lot of money and I have nothing left, so what chance do I have?"

Despite his worries, Antonio was a generous man, who wanted to help his friend.

"You know that all my money is with my boats," he said, "but I will see if I can borrow some for you. Then you can go to visit this woman and win her heart, and perhaps you can marry her."

KEY WORDS

- including
- mess around
- play the fool
- ambition
- grow old (grow-grew-grown)
- nod
- since
- a load of rubbish
- affectionately
- pat ~ on the back

- **speak up** (speak-spoke-spoken)
- **at last**
- **win** (win-won-won)
- **fine**
- **offer**
- **owe**
- **despite** (= in spite of)
- **see if** (see-saw-seen)
- **borrow** (↔ lend)
- **perhaps**

Many miles away, at her home in Belmont, the very same woman, Portia, was speaking to her maid, Nerissa.

"It's all so difficult," complained Portia, "because my father left instructions in his will that I could not choose my own husband, but that a strange kind of contest must take place. All these men come here, wanting to marry me, but I'm not allowed to decide whether I marry them or I don't."

Nerissa laid a comforting hand on her mistress' shoulder and assured her that her father meant well.

"That's why he came up with the three caskets," she said, pointing towards three caskets — one made of gold, the second made of silver, and the third made of lead.

"Whoever reads the messages written on each one must work out the meaning. The man who then chooses the casket that has a picture of you in it will be allowed to marry you."

KEY WORDS

- **mile** (= 1,609 m)
- **the very same**
- **maid**
- **complain**
- **instruction**
- **will**
- **take place** (take-took-taken)
- **be allowed to** + *Verb*
- **decide**
- **whether**
- **lay** (lay-laid-laid)

- **comforting**
- **mistress**
- **assure**
- **mean well** (mean-meant-meant)
- **come up with** (come-came-come)
- **casket**
- **(be) made of**
- **lead**
- **whoever**
- **work out**

Nerissa leaned closer to whisper in Portia's ear. "But tell me, do you like any of the men who have already been here?" Portia groaned, threw back her head and tried to remember them all.

"The Prince of Napoli talked about his horse all the time, and the man who came after him did nothing but frown. The French man thought that he was better than everyone else, and I couldn't even have a conversation with the English man because we didn't understand each other! The Scottish lord was rather violent and liked to hit people, so I didn't think much of him."

Nerissa pressed a hand to her mouth to hide her giggles. "What about the German man who is here now, waiting to choose a casket?"

KEY WORDS

- lean
- whisper
- groan
- throw back one's head (throw-threw-thrown)
- all the time
- do nothing but + *Verb* (do-did-done)
- frown
- have a conversation (have-had-had)
- understand (understand-understood-understood)
- each other

- Scottish
- lord
- rather
- violent
- think much of (think-thought-thought)
- press
- hide (hide-hid-hidden)
- giggle
- what about ~?

Portia got up from her couch and pretended to fall over again. "He is drunk most of the time, and I really don't like him."

"But what if he chooses the right casket?" asked Nerissa, curiously. "Will you disobey your father's wishes and refuse to marry him?" But Portia had a plan to make sure that didn't happen. "Put a glass of wine on the *wrong* casket," she said, "and he will choose that one!"

POP QUIZ

How did Portia plan to make sure that she did not marry the German man?

ⓐ She planned to put a glass of wine on the wrong casket.
ⓑ She planned to prevent him from choosing any casket.

KEY WORDS

- couch
- pretend to + *Verb*
- fall over (fall-fell-fallen)

- be drunk (*cf.* drink(drink-drank-drunk))
- what if ~?
- curiously

- disobey
- refuse
- make sure

Nerissa looked thoughtful. "Do you remember that man called Bassanio who came from Venice? He didn't get as far as choosing the caskets, but he was attractive."

"That's right; he was certainly a handsome man," agreed Portia, looking thoughtful as she remembered Bassanio.

Just then, a servant came in and announced that four men were just leaving, but the Prince of Morocco had just arrived.

Portia threw herself back down on the couch and heaved another sigh. "Will it never end?" she groaned.

KEY WORDS

- thoughtful
- as far as
- attractive
- certainly

- handsome
- agree
- servant
- announce

- heave a sigh
- another
- end

Meanwhile, in the marketplace of Venice, the same handsome Bassanio was talking to a moneylender called Shylock. He was well-known in Venice, since he lent money to people and charged them very high rates of interest. This meant that if someone borrowed money from him, they ended up paying back a lot more than they borrowed in the first place. He was a cruel, selfish man who did not like many people.

"I want to borrow 3,000 ducats," said Bassanio, "and my friend Antonio will make sure that it is paid back in full." Shylock stroked his beard thoughtfully as he replied, "Antonio is a good man, but his ships may get wrecked and then he will have no money."

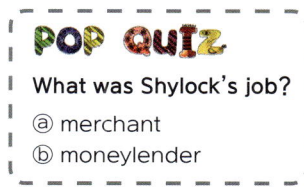

POP QUIZ

What was Shylock's job?

ⓐ merchant

ⓑ moneylender

KEY WORDS

- meanwhile
- marketplace
- moneylender
- charge
- rate of interest

- end up + *Verb*-ing
- pay back
- in the first place
- cruel
- selfish

- ducat
- in full
- stroke
- beard
- thoughtfully

At that moment, Antonio himself came striding along, and Shylock muttered to himself. "I hate Antonio because he lends out money for free, which means that people don't come to borrow it from me and pay me interest on it."

He stopped muttering to himself and said out loud."Ah, Antonio, I was just talking about you. I know that you are willing to make sure that Bassanio's loan is paid back, but why should I lend it to him?"

Antonio really disliked the sly, selfish moneylender, but he was willing to do business for Bassanio's sake.

"If you lend money to your enemy," he said, "then you will find it all the easier to demand a penalty if I fail to pay back the money in time. Don't do it out of love, but rather do it so that you can get your revenge if I don't pay you back what I owe at the right time."

KEY WORDS

- come along
- stride
- mutter to oneself
- for free
- be willing to + *Verb*
- loan
- dislike (↔ like)
- sly
- do business

- for A's sake
- all the
- demand
- penalty
- fail
- in time
- out of love
- get one's revenge
  (get-got-gotten)

- very well
- legally
- write down (write-wrote-written)
- pound (≒ 0.45 kg)
- flesh
- horrible
- confident
- plenty of
- deal

"Very well then," agreed Shylock, "but I want it all legally written down. And if you *do* fail to pay back the money, then the penalty shall be… a pound of your own flesh!"

Nobody but Shylock could have thought of such a horrible penalty, but Antonio was confident that his ships would return with plenty of money within two months.

And so the terrible deal was agreed.

a pound of flesh

There was a fanfare of trumpets as the Prince of Morocco arrived at Portia's great house.

"Please don't turn me down because my skin color is different than yours," begged the prince.

"I don't choose a man because of how he looks," replied Portia. "If I *could* choose, you would stand as good a chance as anyone, but we have to keep to my father's wishes. But remember that if you choose the wrong casket, you can never get married. We'll go to the casket room after dinner."

KEY WORDS

- fanfare
- trumpet
- turn down
- different than[from]

- beg
- stand a chance (stand-stood-stood)
- keep to (keep-kept-kept)
- get married

As Bassanio walked down the street with a crowd of friends, he was busy giving instructions to one of his servants, reminding him to have supper ready by five o'clock since there was an important guest coming to eat with him. *Aha!* Gratiano, the joker, came running and leaping along the road.

"Bassanio," he called, "may I go to Portia's house with you?"

"All right," agreed Bassanio, "but you'll have to do something about your behavior. You're often rude, you behave badly, and you speak too loudly. I don't mind any of these things, but other people might, and I don't want you to ruin my chance with Portia by being a fool."

POP QUIZ

What did Bassanio tell his servant to do?

ⓐ to speak more quietly
ⓑ to have supper ready at five o'clock

KEY WORDS

- a crowd of
- remind
- supper
- joker
- leap
- behavior
- rude
- behave badly
- mind
- ruin

Gratiano put his hands together as though he was praying and forced his face into a serious expression. "I will be as solemn as a priest," he said, "and I will behave with dignity." 📖
Aha!

Bassanio couldn't hold back a smile as he murmured, "We'll see about that."

"But tonight doesn't count," said Gratiano, grinning again.

"Yes, I want you to be wild and entertaining tonight," said Bassanio, nodding, "because some guests are coming to my house who need to be made more cheerful."

"I'll go and look for Lorenzo and the others," said Gratiano, "and we'll come and find you at suppertime."

POP QUIZ

Why did Bassanio want Gratiano to be wild and entertaining?

ⓐ He wanted Gratiano to impress Portia with his jokes.
ⓑ He wanted Gratiano to cheer up his supper guests.

KEY WORDS

- as though
- force
- expression
- priest
- with dignity
- hold back (hold-held-held)
- murmur
- count
- grin
- wild
- entertaining
- cheerful
- look for
- suppertime

Chapter One Comprehension Quiz

A Circle the character who spoke each line.

❶ "I don't choose a man because of how he looks."

Bassanio / Portia / Gratiano

❷ "I want to borrow 3,000 ducats."

Bassanio / Portia / Gratiano

❸ "I will behave with dignity."

Bassanio / Portia / Gratiano

B Fill in each blank with the right word below.

color	casket	fanfare	chance

❶ There was a _____ of trumpets as the Prince of Morocco arrived.

❷ The Prince of Morocco begged Portia not to turn him down because of his skin _____.

❸ If the Prince of Morocco chose the wrong _____, he could never get married.

❹ Portia told the Prince of Morocco that he would stand as good a _____ as anyone.

C Choose the best answer to each question.

❶ Why was being a merchant a "dangerous game"?

a) Many people wanted to kill merchants.

b) Merchants risked everything each time their ships sailed away.

c) Merchants risked drowning as they steered their ships.

d) The goods brought on the ships gave diseases to merchants.

❷ How would Portia's husband be chosen?

a) Her father would write down the name.

b) Her maid would choose a husband for her.

c) Her husband would be the man who chose the right casket.

d) She would choose the man who drew the best picture of her.

❸ Why did Shylock agree to lend the money to Bassanio?

a) Shylock liked Bassanio and wanted to do him a favor.

b) Shylock wanted Antonio to sell some ships to him.

c) Shylock wanted to make everyone love him more.

d) Shylock disliked Antonio and wanted to get revenge on him.

Chapter Two

Plans for Escape

Shylock's daughter, Jessica, was deep in conversation with a young man called Launcelot Gobbo in a quiet corner of Shylock's house. Launcelot was one of Shylock's servants, but he had decided to leave and work for Bassanio instead. "I'm sorry that you're leaving," whispered Jessica. "Our house is such a miserable place, but it was more lively with you around." 📖
Aha!

She handed Launcelot a letter and urged him to hide it away at once.

"I want you to give this letter to Lorenzo. He is one of Bassanio's friends," she went on, keeping her voice low. "Give him this letter now, secretly. And later tonight at Bassanio's I don't want my father to see you talking together."

KEY WORDS

- escape
- be in conversation with
- deep
- instead
- miserable

- lively
- hand
- urge
- at once
- go on (go-went-gone)

Away went Launcelot, leaving Jessica to continue talking to herself. "How terrible is that?" she sighed. "I am ashamed to be my father's child! But although I'm related to him, I don't have to behave like him. Oh, Lorenzo, if you will keep your promise, then I'll end all this trouble by becoming your wife."

KEY WORDS

- ashamed
- although
- be related to
- keep one's promise

Elsewhere in the city of Venice, Gratiano and Lorenzo were
making plans with their friends, Salarino and Salanio.

"We'll creep away at suppertime and go to my house," said
Lorenzo. "We'll disguise ourselves and then come back here
in a little while."

"But we haven't prepared properly!" protested Gratiano.

"He's right," agreed Salarino, "and we haven't discussed who
will carry the torch to light our way along the dark streets."

Lorenzo shook his head at the negative attitude of his
friends. "It's only four o'clock now, so we've still got two
hours to get everything ready."

Just then, Launcelot Gobbo came running down the street, the letter in his hand. He handed it to Lorenzo, who looked at it closely.

"I recognize the handwriting on this letter," he exclaimed. "It's from Jessica."

Launcelot didn't wait to hear what was in the letter, but began to walk away. He was in a hurry to say goodbye to Shylock so that he could eat that night with his new master, Bassanio.

"Wait!" Lorenzo called after him. "Tell Jessica that I will not fail her, but make sure that you tell her privately."

Launcelot nodded and hurried away.

POP QUIZ

How did Lorenzo know that the letter was from Jessica?

ⓐ He recognized the handwriting.
ⓑ The letter smelled of her perfume.

KEY WORDS

- elsewhere
- make a plan
- creep away (creep-crept-crept)
- disguise oneself
- in a little while
- properly

- protest
- discuss
- torch
- negative
- attitude
- get ready

- recognize
- handwriting
- exclaim
- in a hurry master
- privately

A thoughtful smile crossed Lorenzo's face. "I think I know who will carry the torch for us tonight. Go and get ready for our grand performance!"

Salarino and Salanio agreed, and after arranging to meet at Gratiano's house in an hour's time, they rushed away, too.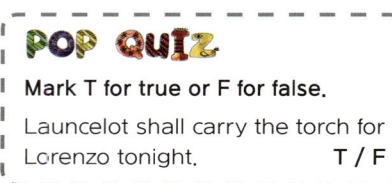

Gratiano nudged Lorenzo and said, "So what did Jessica have to say?"

"She is bringing gold and jewels from her father's house, and will be dressed as a boy when I go to collect her. Jessica shall carry the torch for us tonight!"

POP QUIZ

Mark T for true or F for false.

Launcelot shall carry the torch for Lorenzo tonight.   T / F

KEY WORDS

- cross
- performance
- arrange
- rush away
- nudge
- dress as

- collect
- grumble
- regret
- call for
- invite out to
- respectable

- be about to + *Verb*
- urgently
- safely
- out of the way

Shylock grumbled about Launcelot Gobbo leaving him, and told him that he would regret it. Then, he called for Jessica.

"What do you want?" she said, coming out of the house to where her father and Launcelot stood in the street.

"I have been invited out to supper," explained Shylock, "but I don't really want to go. Bassanio wants me to eat with him, to make our deal respectable. But everything feels strange tonight, as though something is about to happen."

"You must go!" said Jessica urgently, wanting her father to be safely out of the way that night so that she could meet Lorenzo.

"Then I shall leave you with my keys. Jessica, make sure that you lock the doors and don't answer them if anyone comes knocking. Neither should you look out the windows if you hear people in the streets." 📖 Aha!

"If you do look out, you might see something worth looking at," whispered Launcelot, giving Jessica a meaningful look before strolling away down the street.

She knew that he was talking about Lorenzo, and her heart beat a little faster.

"What's he talking about?" snapped Shylock, as he got ready to leave.

"It's just his way of saying goodbye," said Jessica, who wasn't about to tell her father that he was right — something *was* going to happen tonight.

KEY WORDS

- **lock** (↔ unlock)
- **neither**
- **worth**
- **meaningful**
- **stroll**
- **beat** (beat-beat-beaten)
- **snap**

- **not be about to + *Verb***
- **waste**
- **indoors**
- **hunched**
- **figure**
- **disappear** (↔ appear)
- **lose** (lose-lost-lost)

"Launcelot Gobbo is a lazy young man, and I don't mind him going to waste Bassanio's money," said Shylock. "All right, Jessica, you go indoors and I'll leave for the supper party."

Shylock went away down the street, his hunched figure disappearing into the shadows as Jessica watched him go. "Goodbye," she murmured, "and if things work out as I plan, then I have lost a father and you have lost a daughter."

Later that evening Gratiano, Salarino, and Lorenzo waited outside Shylock's house, all wearing masks. Lorenzo knocked at the door and called, "Is there anyone at home?"

"Who is it?" came Jessica's voice from a window above. "I recognize your voice, but I need to be sure that you are who I think you are."

When she was convinced that the masked man below was indeed her lover, Lorenzo, she passed down a casket of jewels and money.

"I'm glad it's dark," she said, "because I don't really want you to see me dressed as a boy." 📖 Aha!

She opened the door and slipped out into the street, bringing more treasure with her. Safely disguised, she carried the torch as she and Lorenzo hurried away with their friends along the dark streets of Venice.

> ## POP QUIZ
> Why didn't Jessica know for sure that it was Lorenzo who came to her house?
> ⓐ He was wearing a mask.
> ⓑ He was disguised as a girl.

KEY WORDS

- convinced
- indeed
- pass
- slip

At Portia's house in Belmont, the Prince of Morocco was ready to make his choice, hoping to win Portia as his wife. "Draw aside the curtains and show him the three caskets," Portia ordered her servant.

The first casket was made of gold, and written on it were these words: *If you choose me, you will get what many men desire.*

The second casket was made of silver, and written on it were these words: *If you choose me, you shall get as much as you deserve.*

The third casket was made of dull lead, and written on it were these words: *If you choose me, you must give and risk everything you have.*

KEY WORDS

- **make a choice**
- **draw** (draw-drew-drawn)
- **aside**
- **desire**
- **deserve**
- **dull**

"One of them contains a picture of me," explained Portia, "and if you choose that one, then I shall be your wife."

The prince read the words again, muttering to himself, and trying to work out what the words meant so that he could make up his mind. At last, he made his decision.

"Gold is the most precious thing of these three," he declared, "so that must be the one that contains Portia's picture."

A servant handed him the key to the casket, and the prince unlocked it.

Inside, he found a picture of a skull, and a scroll which told him all that he needed to know.

Not everything that looks beautiful is gold, it said. *Don't judge what is inside by what is on the outside.*

Sick with disappointment, the prince and all his servants left Portia's house, never to return.

POP QUIZ

Why did the Prince of Morocco decide to choose the gold casket?

ⓐ It was the biggest casket.

ⓑ It was made of the most precious metal.

KEY WORDS

- contain
- make up one's mind
- make a decision
- precious
- declare

- skull
- scroll
- judge
- with disappointment

Next to arrive was the Prince of Spain, who had arrived to take his chance and to try to choose the correct casket.

He bowed low to Portia and said, "I have promised three things. First, I will never tell anyone which casket I choose today. Second, if I fail to choose the right casket, then I agree never to get married. Third, if I make the wrong choice, then I will leave you at once."

"Everyone must make these three promises in order to take part in the contest," Portia reminded him, "so you must make your choice, just like everyone else."

The prince read the writing on each casket carefully, and in the end he decided to choose… the silver one.

Inside was a picture of a fool, and another message: *Real silver is purified by fire, and good judgement is learned with difficulty. Some people appear to be wise, but are foolish.* Accepting his defeat, the prince left with his servants, never to return.

Just as Portia was sitting back against her cushions with a sigh, a servant hurried in with news of another arrival.

A ship had brought another man to seek Portia's hand in marriage, and this time his name was one that she recognized: Bassanio.

POP QUIZ

What was Portia doing when Bassanio arrived?

ⓐ sitting back against the cushions
ⓑ looking out of the window

KEY WORDS

- take one's chance
- bow low
- in order to + *Verb*
- take part in
- in the end
- purify
- judgement

- with difficulty
- foolish
- accept
- defeat
- arrival (*cf.* arrive)
- seek one's hand in marriage
  (seek-sought-sought)

A Fill in each blank with the right word below.

| disappeared | whispered | grumbled | invited |

❶ Shylock _____ about Launcelot Gobbo leaving him.

❷ Bassanio _____ Shylock to his house for supper.

❸ Launcelot _____ some information into Jessica's ear.

❹ Shylock _____ into the shadows as he went away down the street.

B Circle the right word for each underlined part.

❶ Everyone must make (<u>two / three / four</u>) promises to take part in the (<u>contest / marriage / journey</u>).

❷ Real silver is purified by (<u>fire / ice / gold</u>), and good judgement is learned with (<u>age / study / difficulty</u>).

❸ Accepting his (<u>reward / wife / defeat</u>), the Prince of Spain left with his (<u>money / servants / casket</u>), never to return.

❹ A (<u>carriage / ship / horse</u>) had brought another man to seek Portia's (<u>ring / promise / hand</u>) in marriage.

C Choose the best answer to each question.

❶ Why was Launcelot in a hurry to leave after delivering the letter?

a) He wanted to start working for Bassanio as soon as possible.

b) He thought that Lorenzo might be angry with him for delivering the letter.

c) He knew that Shylock was looking for him and he wanted to hide.

d) He guessed that the letter contained bad news from Jessica.

❷ What words were found inside the gold casket?

a) *Not everything that looks beautiful is gold.*

b) *If you choose me, you will get what many men desire.*

c) *Some people appear to be wise, but are foolish.*

d) *If you choose me, you shall get as much as you deserve.*

D Put the sentences in order.

❶ Lorenzo knocked at the door of Shylock's house.

❷ Jessica passed down a casket of jewels and money.

❸ Jessica called out from an upstairs window.

❹ Jessica carried a torch as the friends hurried away.

_____ → _____ → _____ → _____

Chapter Three

A Choice and a Promise

Back in Venice, the streets were filled with news and everyone was talking about the things that had happened. Bassanio and Gratiano had sailed away to Belmont and Shylock had demanded that their ship must be searched, because he thought that Lorenzo and Jessica might be on board. But the ship had already sailed away by the time he got some men together, and Lorenzo and Jessica had disappeared.

Shylock was so furious at their disappearance that he went around the streets shouting about it like a mad man. He did not know whether they were with Bassanio or not, but he kept hearing news about all the money that Jessica was spending. One man told him that Jessica had given a sailor Shylock's most precious ring, given to him by his wife, in exchange for a tame monkey.

Shylock grew angrier and angrier as time went on.

KEY WORDS

- be filled with
- on board
- furious
- disappearance

- mad
- sailor
- in exchange for
- tame

- angrier
- as time goes on

But there was worse news for Antonio, since there was a rumor that one of his ships had sunk, along with all the goods on board. Without those goods, he would make no money… and without money, how would he pay back the debt he owed to Shylock?

Shylock rubbed his hands together greedily at this news, determined to keep to the agreement if Antonio could not pay what he owed.

"It will be my revenge for all the times that he has laughed at me and got in the way of my deals," said Shylock, happy to receive some good news at last.

"Surely you will not really do it?" people asked.

But Shylock's eyes glittered with greed and revenge as he nodded his head and insisted, "Of course I will do it. I will take a pound of that man's flesh!"

KEY WORDS

- worse
- rumor
- sink (sink-sank-sunk)
- along with
- debt
- rub
- greedily

- (be) determined to + *Verb*
- agreement
- laugh at
- get in the way of
- receive
- surely
- glitter

- greed
- insist
- of course
- company
- bear (bear-bore-borne)

In Belmont, Portia was enjoying Bassanio's company, and
Nerissa was enjoying the company of his friend, Gratiano.
Portia liked Bassanio so much that she didn't want him to
make his choice too quickly, for if he chose the wrong casket,
then he would have to leave.

"I'd love you to stay here a month or more before you
choose," she said as he stood before her with Gratiano at his
side. "I wish that I could tell you which is the correct casket
to choose, but I must not."

"I can't bear to wait any longer," groaned Bassanio. "I love
you, so lead me to the caskets at once."

"Everyone, stand back while he makes his choice," ordered Portia, "and let us have some music!"

Her musicians played and sang while Bassanio muttered to himself about the caskets, trying to decide which one to choose and knowing that his whole future depended on this one decision.

"People are easily deceived by appearances," he said at last, "so I choose this dull casket of lead."

When he was handed the key and opened the casket, he found a picture of Portia and a message which said: *You didn't choose on looks alone, so you may claim your lady with a kiss*.

Bassanio smiled, and so did Portia, as they moved toward one another and kissed tenderly.

POP QUIZ

Which casket did Bassanio choose?

ⓐ silver

ⓑ lead

KEY WORDS

- depend on
- deceive
- appearance
- claim

- one another
- tenderly
- whatever
- ever

- give away (give-gave-given)
- unless
- clap one's hands

"I hope that I am everything you hope for, and more," said Portia. "Whatever was mine is now yours — my house, my servants and myself."

She handed Bassanio a ring, and urged him to always wear it, saying, "It shows that I am yours. If you ever lose it or give it away, it will be a sign that your love for me has gone."

"I promise that this ring will not leave my hand unless I am dead," said Bassanio, slipping it onto his finger.

Portia's servant, Nerissa, clapped her hands and cried, "We are so happy for you both!"

But Portia was not the only one who had been impressed by the handsome visitors. Nerissa and Gratiano had been growing closer and closer as the days went on and now it was time to speak up.

"When you two get married, may I also be married at the same time?" asked Gratiano.

"Of course you may get yourself a wife," said Bassanio, surprised.

"I have already found one," admitted Gratiano. "While you were busy choosing the correct casket, my fortune depended on it, too, for Nerissa agreed to marry me, provided that you won Portia as your own." Aha!

Everybody laughed and smiled and patted each other on the back. Gratiano even wanted to place a bet with Bassanio about who would have the first son.

KEY WORDS

- be impressed by
- at the same time
- admit
- fortune
- provided (that)
- place a bet

Just then, Lorenzo, Jessica, and Salanio arrived. Lorenzo and Jessica hadn't been on Bassanio's ship after all, but had made their own escape from Venice and at last made their way to Belmont.

Bassanio was pleased to welcome his friends and introduce them to Portia.

"I didn't plan to come and see you," admitted Lorenzo, "but I met Salanio on the way, and he begged me to come."

"I certainly did," agreed Salanio, "and here's the reason why I wanted him to be here." With a solemn face, he handed Bassanio a letter from Antonio.

Nerissa took Jessica to one side and greeted her while the men wondered what was in Antonio's letter.

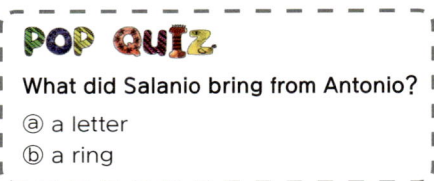

POP QUIZ

What did Salanio bring from Antonio?

ⓐ a letter
ⓑ a ring

KEY WORDS

- after all
- make one's escape
- make one's way
- introduce
- on the way

- reason
- greet
- wonder
- go pale
- in despair

- unpleasant
- wealth
- dear
- every single

"Bassanio, you have gone pale!" said Portia, worried for her future husband. "Only the news of a friend's death could make you look so white. Please tell me what's wrong." Bassanio shook his head in despair and said, "It's the most unpleasant thing I've ever read. All my own wealth that I have told you about was borrowed by my dear friend from a moneylender, and now he has lost everything. Every single one of his ships has sunk."

"How much does he owe?" asked Portia, thinking of her own wealth and how she might be able to help.

"Three thousand ducats," answered Bassanio.

"Then pay back six thousand, twelve thousand, even thirty-six thousand," said Portia. "Bassanio, let's get married quickly and then you can go to Venice to get everything sorted out before returning to me with a peaceful heart."

"My father says that he does not want Antonio's money," said Jessica, "and he would rather have Antonio's flesh than twenty times the money."

After the excitement of a double wedding, it was quiet in Portia's house when Bassanio and Gratiano left. Lorenzo and Jessica stayed, concerned for Portia and how she would bear the absence of her new husband, but she had plans of her own.

"I will live in silent prayer and contemplation until they return," she announced. "Only Nerissa shall keep me company, and we shall stay in the monastery a couple of miles away until the men return. Lorenzo, you and Jessica shall run my household while I am gone."

Lorenzo and Jessica were glad to take on the responsibility, and they hurried away to see what needed to be done.

POP QUIZ

What did Portia want Bassanio to do before he went back to Venice?

ⓐ to marry her
ⓑ to learn about the law

KEY WORDS

- be able to + *Verb*
- sort out
- would rather ... (than ~)
- times
- excitement

- double wedding
- absence
- contemplation
- keep ~ company
- monastery

- run a household
- take on
- responsibility

But Portia did not intend to hide away in the monastery; she had a plan that would allow her and Nerissa to see their husbands again much sooner than they expected. She sent a servant to take a letter to her cousin, a Doctor of Law named Doctor Bellario. 🌐

"Bring whatever he gives you to the public ferry that goes to Venice," she told the servant. "I shall be waiting there for you."

Nerissa was puzzled, especially when Portia explained that their husbands would not recognize them because they would be dressed as men.

"But why shall we dress up and deceive them?" asked Nerissa.

"I'll tell you everything in the coach, which is waiting at the gate," said Portia, urgently. "We must hurry, for we have to travel twenty miles today."

KEY WORDS

- intend to + *Verb*
- expect
- public

- ferry
- puzzled
- especially

- dress up
- coach

The Duke of Venice looked around the court of justice at the people gathered there. Antonio was there, with Bassanio and his friends, and other members of the court were present to witness the events of the day.

"Antonio, I feel sorry for you," began the Duke, "for your enemy, Shylock, has no pity or mercy."

"I know you have tried to persuade him to be less harsh," said Antonio, "but the law must stand and I will be patient and quiet while he rages."

Shylock was called in and he stood in the center of the room in his black robes like a hungry crow, greedy for scraps of flesh.

POP QUIZ

What did the Duke ask Shylock to do?
ⓐ to kill Antonio
ⓑ to forgive Antonio

KEY WORDS

- Duke
- court of justice
- gather
- present
- witness
- pity
- mercy

- persuade
- harsh
- patient
- rage
- robe(s)
- crow
- greedy for

- scrap
- booming
- matter
- forgive (forgive-forgave-forgiven)
- glare at
- hatred

"Shylock," said the Duke in a booming voice, "we expect that you will take this matter as far as you can, but we also hope that you will show mercy in the end. We hope that you will forgive Antonio, especially since he has had so much bad luck already."

"I've already told you that I intend to take what he owes me," said Shylock as he glared at Antonio, hatred in his eyes. "I'd rather have the flesh than the money. After all, some people like one thing and some like another; there doesn't have to be a reason behind it."

"That's no explanation for your cruelty!" Bassanio cried. "You don't have to kill something just because you don't like it."

Antonio grabbed his friend's arm to restrain him and said, "It's not worth arguing with Shylock. He's like a mountain that cannot be moved, no matter how much you may try."

Bassanio offered Shylock all the extra money that Portia had given him, but Shylock refused it.

"How do you expect anyone ever to show you mercy, since you don't show it to anyone else?" asked the Duke.

Shylock shrugged and took out a knife from his cloak.

"I'd rather see justice done than mercy given," he said, and he began to sharpen the knife.

KEY WORDS

- explanation
- cruelty
- grab
- restrain
- argue with
- no matter how
- extra
- shrug
- cloak
- sharpen

A Mark T for true or F for false.

❶ Portia told Lorenzo that she was going to Venice.   T   F

❷ Nerissa married Gratiano before he left with Bassanio.   T   F

❸ Doctor Bellario was Portia's cousin.   T   F

❹ Portia asked Doctor Bellario to run the household while she was gone.   T   F

B Fill in each blank with the right word below.

musicians	hands	caskets	appearances

❶ The _____ played and sang while Bassanio muttered to himself.

❷ Bassanio decided that people are easily deceived by _____.

❸ Bassanio took some time to decide which of the _____ to choose.

❹ Nerissa clapped her _____ because she was happy for Portia and Bassanio.

C Choose the best answer to each question.

❶ What did Shylock want from Antonio if he could not pay the debt?

a) a pound of Antonio's flesh

b) all of Antonio's ships

c) all of Antonio's clothes

d) Antonio's house

❷ Why did Bassanio choose the lead casket?

a) He knew that the people before him had chosen gold and silver.

b) He chose the casket that Portia told him to choose.

c) He thought that Portia was dull and unattractive, like the lead casket.

d) He knew that people judge others by the way they look instead of what they are like inside.

❸ Why did the Duke of Venice feel sorry for Antonio?

a) because Antonio had lost his ships

b) because Antonio had no friends

c) because Antonio's enemy, Shylock, was not merciful

d) because Antonio wanted to get married but had no woman to marry

Chapter Four

A Clever Lawyer

The rasping, scraping sound of the knife being sharpened filled the courtroom as Nerissa burst in, dressed as a lawyer's clerk. She bowed, and handed a letter to the Duke, who frowned as he read it.

"I was expecting Doctor Bellario," he said, "but he has sent us a different lawyer — a young, intelligent man."

Just as he was speaking, Portia entered the courtroom… dressed as a young, intelligent male lawyer!

The Duke welcomed her and Portia stepped closer to Shylock, studying this man who was causing so much trouble to her husband and his friend.

KEY WORDS

- rasping
- scraping
- courtroom

- **burst in** (burst-burst-burst)
- **clerk**
- **intelligent**

- **male** (*cf.* female)
- **study**
- **cause**

"I know all about the agreement between Shylock and the merchant, Antonio," she said, "but we cannot change the law, since Antonio signed the agreement. Therefore, we need Shylock to be merciful."

"Why should I be merciful?" snapped Shylock, waving his knife around so that it glinted in a shaft of sunlight.

"Because mercy blesses both the one who gives it and the one who receives it," said Portia. "It shows the true worth of a man. Kings demonstrate it, and God himself is merciful. If we all got what we deserved, then none of us would be saved from the things we do wrong."

"I don't care," snapped Shylock, who was getting angry now. "I just want the law to be fulfilled."

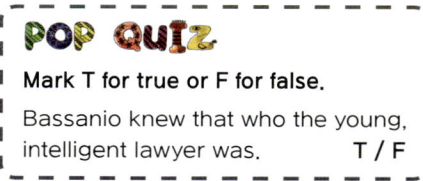

POP QUIZ

Mark T for true or F for false.
Bassanio knew that who the young, intelligent lawyer was.   T / F

KEY WORDS

- therefore
- merciful
- wave
- glint

- a shaft of sunlight
- bless
- demonstrate
- fulfill

- amount
- snarl
- pay off
- either A or B

"Can Antonio not pay the money?" asked Portia, glancing at Bassanio, who had no idea who she was.

"Yes," Bassanio cried, "for I have twice the amount here, and will get ten times more if I need to."

"It was Antonio who signed the loan agreement," snarled Shylock. "I don't want you to pay off his debt. I want him to either pay it himself or give me the pound of flesh that I am owed."

"If Shylock doesn't want the money," Bassanio said to Portia, "can't you bend the law a little to bring about the outcome that is truly right?"

"No," said Portia, sternly, "for the law cannot be changed, as I have said. If we change it now, then others will try to do the same in the future."

She looked closely at the written agreement, and everyone except Shylock and Antonio gasped as she said, "Shylock may cut off a pound of Antonio's flesh, close to his heart."

Shylock waved his knife around and exclaimed, "What an excellent lawyer you are!"

KEY WORDS

- **bend the law** (bend-bent-bent)
- **bring about** (bring-brought-brought)

- outcome
- sternly

- except
- gasp

68 • Chapter Four

Portia instructed Antonio to open his shirt, so that Shylock could take the flesh.

"Shylock," she said, "do you have some scales so that we can weigh the flesh, and a doctor to stop him bleeding to death?"

"I have the scales," said Shylock, "but the agreement does not require me to provide a doctor."

Antonio had very little to say as he grasped Bassanio's hand and begged him not to grieve.

"After all," he declared, "it is better to die now than to live a miserable life as a poor man."

Bassanio was terribly upset at the thought of losing his dearest friend. "I now have a wife whom I love dearly," he wept, "but I would rather lose her than see you die, my dear friend."

POP QUIZ

What did Portia ask Shylock to provide?

ⓐ scales and a doctor
ⓑ a shirt and a knife

KEY WORDS

- instruct
- scales
- **bleed to death** (bleed-bled-bled)
- require

- provide
- grasp
- grieve
- upset

- dearest
- dearly
- **weep** (weep-wept-wept)

Portia, safe in her disguise, raised her eyebrows. "I'm sure your wife wouldn't be very pleased to hear that!"

"And I too have a wife whom I love," said Gratiano, "but I wish that she were in heaven so that she could call on heavenly powers to change Shylock's mind."

Nerissa, also in disguise, folded her arms and glared at her husband, Gratiano, saying, "It's a good thing that she's not here, or there would be trouble in your house!"

"We're wasting time." complained Shylock, angry at the delay.

"You may have your pound of flesh," Portia announced, "but you are not permitted to take anything else. If you take a single drop of blood, then you're breaking the law, and everything you own will belong to the state of Venice."

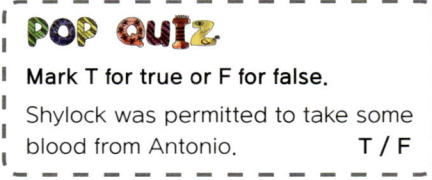

POP QUIZ

Mark T for true or F for false.

Shylock was permitted to take some blood from Antonio.   T / F

KEY WORDS

- raise one's eyebrow(s)
- heaven (*cf.* heavenly)
- call on
- fold one's arms
- delay
- permit

- drop
- break (break-broke-broken)
- belong to
- state
- stun
- silence

- realize
- scowl
- stamp
- forward
- firmly

A stunned silence fell across the courtroom as everyone realized how clever Portia was being.

"You really *are* an excellent lawyer!" said Gratiano.

Shylock scowled and stamped about, and then said, "All right, then; pay me three times the money that is owed instead, and I'll let Antonio go."

Bassanio hurried forward with the money, but Portia stopped him.

"No, Shylock must have what he asked for," she said, firmly. "Take the pound of flesh, Shylock, but make sure that it is exactly a pound. If it is any more or less, even by the weight of a hair, then you will be the one who dies."

Shylock tried to get himself out of trouble.

"It's all right," he insisted, "I'll just take the original amount of money that was owed. Three thousand ducats will be plenty and then we can all leave the court happy."

"You have already refused it in front of everyone," Portia reminded him, "so it's the pound of flesh or nothing."

"Forget the whole thing, then." shouted Shylock. "I'm leaving!"

He tried to walk out of the courtroom, but Portia glanced at the guards and nodded, and they leaped in front of Shylock to bar his way.

"Not so fast," said Portia, shaking her head. "You have tried to cause the death of another person. According to the laws of Venice, the penalty for this is to give half of your wealth to Antonio and the other half to the state. Only the Duke can decide whether to spare your life, so you'd better kneel before him and start begging."

Shylock bowed his head but his old knees would not permit him to get down on the floor before the Duke.

"You will see how different we are," said the Duke, kindly, "for I'll pardon you before you even ask me to. You do not need to die, but you must give half of your wealth to Antonio and pay the other half to the City of Venice as a fine."

POP QUIZ

Who had the power to spare Shylock's life?

ⓐ the Duke
ⓑ Antonio

KEY WORDS

- get out of trouble
- original
- plenty
- in front of
- guard
- bar
- according to
- spare
- kneel (kneel-kneeled/knelt-kneeled/knelt)
- get down
- pardon

"I'll give my half to Lorenzo," said Antonio. "Please let Shylock keep the rest until he dies, but I think you should make him write a will, leaving everything he owns to Jessica after he dies."

So Shylock was made to write a will, in which he would leave everything he owned to Jessica.

Since he was such a generous man, Antonio decided to do something very kind and merciful, which Shylock did not deserve.

Antonio decided to leave his half of Shylock's money with Shylock for now. Shylock could keep it until his death, but he must then give it to Lorenzo.

Having agreed to this generous plan, the Duke and his servants left the courthouse, but Bassanio pulled Portia aside — not recognizing her, of course.

POP QUIZ

What did Portia ask Bassanio to give her?

ⓐ his ring
ⓑ some money

KEY WORDS

▪ for now ▪ pull aside ▪ go cold

"You have really helped my friend and me today," he said, "so please let me pay you the three thousand ducats that were owed to Shylock."

"I don't need your money," said Portia, hiding a smile, "but I would like that ring that you wear on your finger."

Bassanio went cold as he remembered his promise to Portia that the ring would never leave his finger.

Why had the lawyer asked for the one thing that he could not give away?

"This ring?" he said, pretending to laugh about it. "You really don't want it, since it's worth nothing."

"I've set my mind on it, and will accept nothing else," insisted Portia, testing Bassanio to see if he would keep his word about the ring.

Bassanio refused to let her have it, and Portia pretended to be offended as she walked away.

"Bassanio, you should let the lawyer have the ring," said Antonio. "I know that you promised your wife you would keep that ring, but surely this is more important."

"Oh, all right, then," sighed Bassanio as he slipped the ring from his finger before he could change his mind.

"Gratiano, run after the lawyer and give him this ring. In the morning, we'll all go back to Belmont and I will see my beautiful Portia again."

So Bassanio gave up his special ring to Portia, and when Gratiano delivered it, Nerissa persuaded him to give her *his* ring, too.

KEY WORDS

- set one's mind on (set-set-set)
- be offended
- run after
- give A up (to B)
- deliver

A Connect each character and each line correctly.

❶

❷

- a) "I just want the law to be fulfilled."

- b) "The law cannot be changed."

- c) "Can Antonio not pay the money?"

- d) "What an excellent lawyer you are!"

B Fill in each blank with the right word below.

sighed	pretended	promised	delivered

❶ Portia _____ to be offended as she walked away.

❷ Bassanio _____ his wife that he would keep the ring.

❸ Bassanio _____ as he slipped the ring from his finger.

❹ Gratiano _____ the ring to Portia.

C Solve the crossword puzzle.

Across

❶ Shylock wanted to take the o_____ amount of money that was owed.

❸ Portia asked Shylock to be m_____.

❺ Antonio did not want a m_____ life as a poor man.

Down

❷ The Duke described the new lawyer as young and i_____.

❹ Portia said that Bassanio's wife would not be p_____ to hear his words.

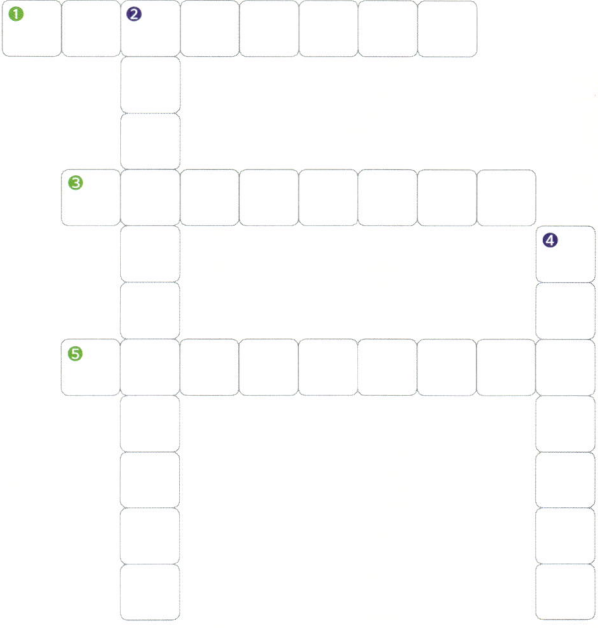

Everything Is Revealed

Chapter Five

It was a beautiful, moonlit night at Portia's house, and
Lorenzo and Jessica were walking in the garden together.
"How bright the moon is," said Lorenzo, "and what a
beautiful night it is."
They chatted together, teasing one another and laughing
until they were interrupted by approaching footsteps.

A servant stepped out of the shadows, with news that Portia would return from the monastery at dawn.

Of course, Lorenzo and Jessica had no idea that Portia had been on a trip to Venice and had saved Antonio from Shylock's knife.

They were just discussing what needed to be done to welcome Portia home when more news arrived, this time from Bassanio, announcing that he too would arrive in the morning with Antonio.

Jessica wanted to go into the house and get busy, but Lorenzo wanted to stay outdoors a little longer, so he ordered that the musicians play inside the house, but loud enough that they could hear it in the garden. He and Jessica sat down on a grassy bank in the moonlight and looked up at the stars as the gentle music played.

KEY WORDS

- reveal
- moonlit
- chat
- tease

- interrupt
- approach
- footstep
- at dawn

- outdoors (↔ indoors)
- grassy
- bank
- gentle

Not far away, Portia and Nerissa approached the house, walking carefully along the road.

"That light we see is from my house," Portia pointed out.

"One small candle shines a long way on a dark night, just as a kind act shines in a wicked world."

She tilted her head to one side, listening to the music, which sounded so much sweeter at night because everything else was silent.

Lorenzo sat up with a start and said, "I'm sure I can hear Portia's voice."

Then, he saw the shapes of Portia and Nerissa appearing from the darkness, and leaped up to greet them.

"We have been at the monastery, praying for our husbands," explained Portia. "Are they home yet?"

"Not yet," said Lorenzo, "but we've had a message to say that they are coming soon."

POP QUIZ

Why did Lorenzo sit up with a start?

ⓐ He heard Portia's voice.
ⓑ He heard some music.

KEY WORDS

- act
- wicked
- tilt

- sit up (sit-sat-sat)
- with a start
- darkness

- yet
- all along

Portia instructed Nerissa to go indoors and tell the servants to act as though the two of them had been at home all along. They didn't want Bassanio and Gratiano to know that they had been away anywhere, and they certainly didn't want anyone to know about their clever plan to save Antonio's life.

A fanfare of trumpets announced Bassanio's arrival, and
Lorenzo also promised to keep their secret safe, even though
he didn't know where they had really been.
"The night is looking a little paler, like a gloomy day,"
observed Portia, as Bassanio, Antonio and Gratiano arrived.
Portia welcomed them all, including Antonio, who did not
realize that he had already met her in the courtroom. She
acted as though this was their first meeting.

Nerissa stepped out of the house and was soon quarrelling with Gratiano.

"I gave it to the lawyer's clerk!" Gratiano said. "I didn't realize that you would be so upset."

"What's going on?" asked Portia. "Why are you two quarrelling already?"

"It's just about a silly old ring that she gave me, with '*Love me and leave me not*' written on it," explained Gratiano.

"It doesn't matter how much it was worth, or what was written on it," Nerissa cried. "You promised to wear it until you died, and that even then you said that it would lie with you in your grave, but I expect you gave it to another girl."

"Actually, he was a young man — a sort of boy — around the same height as you," said Gratiano. "He begged for it so hard that I couldn't say no."

KEY WORDS

- keep a secret
- paler
- gloomy
- observe
- quarrel with

- silly
- lie (lie-lay-lain) (*cf.* lie(lie-lied-lied))
- grave
- a sort of
- height

"You were wrong to do that," said Portia. "You should never have parted with your wife's gift so easily. If *my* husband gave away the ring that he promised to wear forever, I would be really angry."

Bassanio knew that he was in trouble and he whispered to Antonio, "Perhaps I should have cut off my hand and swear that I lost the ring in a fight."

"Bassanio *did* give his ring away, to the lawyer," said Gratiano, accusingly.

"Which ring did you give to the lawyer, Bassanio?" asked Portia. "Not the one that I gave you, I hope."

Bassanio hung his head and held out his hand. "I can't lie," he said. "As you can see, the ring is gone."

"Well, I won't be joining you in our marriage bed until I see that ring again," said Portia, angrily.

"And the same goes for me," said Nerissa, folding her arms and scowling at Gratiano.
Aha!

KEY WORDS

- part with
- be in trouble
- should have + *p.p.*
- swear (swear-swore-sworn)
- accusingly

- hang one's head (hang-hung-hung)
- hold out
- be gone
- marriage bed
- unwillingly

"If you knew why I gave it away, and how unwillingly, you would not be angry," said Bassanio.

"If you had known how precious it was, or how much it meant to me, then you would not have parted with it," replied Portia. "I expect you gave yours to a woman, too."

"No, I honestly didn't! It was a Doctor of Law, who refused three thousand ducats but begged for the ring instead. I did say no, but he went away unhappy. I felt so ashamed after the way he saved Antonio that I changed my mind and gave him the ring after all. If you had been there, Portia, you would have told me to give the ring away."

Of course, Portia *had* been there, and she knew exactly what had happened, but she said, "That doctor had better not come anywhere near my house! If he does, I'll give him everything he asks for, including my body and my bed. You'd better watch out, Bassanio, or I might fall in love with him if you leave me, even for a night."

"And if his clerk comes, then I might love him too," Nerissa joined in.

"This is all my fault," said Antonio, shaking his head. "I faithfully swear that Bassanio will make sure he never breaks another promise, if you will only forgive him this time."

KEY WORDS

- honestly
- had better not + *Verb*
- watch out
- fall in love with
- fault
- faithfully

Portia pretended to think carefully about it, and at last she said, "Very well, then, give him *this* ring, and make sure that he looks after it better than he did the other one."

She handed Antonio the very same ring that Bassanio had given to her when she was disguised as a Doctor of Law. Antonio passed it to Bassanio, who looked at it in astonishment and said, "But it's the same one that I gave to the doctor!"

KEY WORDS

▪ look after

▪ in astonishment

"And I got it from *him*," said Portia, raising her eyebrows. "In fact, that doctor has slept in my bed."

"And the doctor's clerk has slept in *my* bed," declared Nerissa.

Gratiano was furious, and shouted, "Do you mean that you have both cheated on us by falling in love with other men while we were away?"

Portia couldn't keep the secret any longer, and cried, "The good news is that *I* was the Doctor of Law, and Nerissa was my clerk. Antonio, I have even better news for you: three of your ships came home safely after all!"

Bassanio, Gratiano, and Antonio were speechless with surprise when they realized just what had been going on. "You have given me my life back with this good news!" exclaimed Antonio.

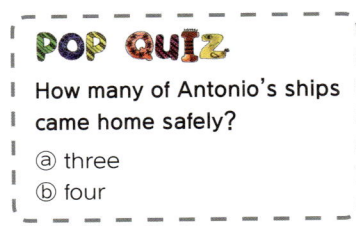

POP QUIZ

How many of Antonio's ships came home safely?
ⓐ three
ⓑ four

KEY WORDS

- in fact
- cheat on
- speechless
- with surprise
- as usual
- as long as

"Lorenzo, there's news for you and Jessica, too," Portia went on. "Shylock has signed an agreement to say that after he dies, he will leave everything he owns to both of you. Let's go inside and share the full story, for there are lots of questions to ask, and to be answered."

Gratiano had the last word, as usual, as he declared, "My first question is to Nerissa. It's almost morning, so shall we go to bed now, or shall we wait until the next night comes? As long as I live, I will keep Nerissa's ring safe and never give it away again."

Chapter
Five **Comprehension Quiz**

A Connect each character and each line correctly.

❶

• a) "That doctor had better not come anywhere near my house."

❷

• b) "It doesn't matter how much it was worth."

❸

• c) "He begged for it so hard that I couldn't say no."

B Fill in each blank with the right word below.

house	bank	trip

❶ Lorenzo and Jessica had no idea that Portia had been on a _____ to Venice.

❷ Lorenzo and Jessica sat on a grassy _____ in the moonlight.

❸ Portia saw a light coming from her _____.

C Choose the best answer to each question.

❶ Why did Portia act as though she did not know Antonio?

a) She had never met him before.

b) She wanted to be rude to him.

c) She did not recognize him.

d) She didn't want anyone to know that she had been at the court.

❷ Why did Bassanio "hang his head"?

a) He was ashamed that he had given the ring away.

b) He was looking for the ring on the ground.

c) He was angry with Portia for questioning him.

d) He had told a lie and was trying to hide it.

❸ What did Portia say might happen if the Doctor of Law came to her house?

a) She might chase him away.

b) She might hurt him.

c) She might fall in love with him.

d) She might ask him to teach her about the law.

Let's Review the Story

Fill in the blanks to review the story.

Title: The _____ of Venice

Chapter 1: _____ needs some money to impress _____. He and his friend, the _____ Antonio, borrow money from the _____, Shylock. Antonio promises that if he fails to pay back the money, he will give Shylock a pound of his own _____.

Chapter 2: Shylock's daughter, _____, runs away with her lover, Lorenzo. In Belmont, men who want to marry Portia must choose the right _____ with the picture of _____ in it.

Chapter 3: Bassanio and Gratiano go to _____. Bassanio chooses the correct _____. He marries Portia, and Gratiano marries Portia's maid, _____. They hear about Antonio's situation. Bassanio and Gratiano return to _____. Portia and Nerissa _____ themselves as men, and follow them there.

Chapter 4: Portia pretends to be a Doctor of _____. She agrees that Shylock can take exactly one pound of _____ from Antonio, but nothing more. Shylock realizes that is impossible. Bassanio gives his _____ to the Doctor of Law… who is _____ in disguise!

Chapter 5: Everyone returns to _____. Portia pretends to be _____ that Bassanio has given his ring away, but she finally admits that she was the _____ of Law. Bassanio promises to be faithful in future, and Antonio hears that his _____ have not sunk after all.

Let's Think & Talk

Think about the following questions and answer them freely.

❶ Why did Portia's father try to choose his daughter's husband by using caskets made of gold, silver and lead? Organize the words written on each box and tell us the meaning.

❷ Tell us your opinion about the verdict that Portia in disguise gave Shylock in court. Tell us what verdict you would give if you were a lawyer.

❸ After the trial, Bassanio handed over the ring that Portia had given him to Portia in disguise because of Antonio's persuasion. If you had been in Bassanio's shoes, would you have kept your pledge of love or given the ring to follow your friend's opinion?

❹ Organize the part in which in the court Portia in disguise talked about "mercy" and let us know your thoughts about "mercy" and how much you think mercy can be permitted by law.

Let's Review the Story

Title: The _Merchant_ of Venice

Chapter 1: _Bassanio_ needs some money to impress _Portia_. He and his friend, the _merchant_ Antonio, borrow money from the _moneylender_, Shylock. Antonio promises that if he fails to pay back the money, he will give Shylock a pound of his own _flesh_.

Chapter 2: Shylock's daughter, _Jessica_, runs away with her lover, Lorenzo. In Belmont, men who want to marry Portia must choose the right _casket_ with the picture of _Portia_ in it.

Chapter 3: Bassanio and Gratiano go to _Belmont_. Bassanio chooses the correct _casket_. He marries Portia, and Gratiano marries Portia's maid, _Nerissa_. They hear about Antonio's situation. Bassanio and Gratiano return to _Venice_. Portia and Nerissa _disguise_ themselves as men, and follow them there.

Chapter 4: Portia pretends to be a Doctor of _Law_. She agrees that Shylock can take exactly one pound of _flesh_ from Antonio, but nothing more. Shylock realizes that is impossible. Bassanio gives his _ring_ to the Doctor of Law… who is _Portia_ in disguise!

Chapter 5: Everyone returns to _Belmont_. Portia pretends to be _angry_ that Bassanio has given his ring away, but she finally admits that she was the _Doctor_ of Law. Bassanio promises to be faithful in future, and Antonio hears that his _ships_ have not sunk after all.

Smart Readers: **Wise** & **Wide**

After-reading Test

- **The Merchant of Venice**
- **Level 6**
- **27 Questions**

  (Vocabulary 6 / Reading Comprehension 16 /

  Sentence Structure & Grammar 5)

The Merchant of Venice After-reading Test

1. What does "solemn" mean?
   ① ugly   ② narrow
   ③ angry   ④ serious

2. What does "grieve" mean?
   ① take revenge   ② be angry
   ③ be very sad   ④ get married

3. Which of the following pair has the wrong past tense form of the verb?
   ① mean – meant
   ② creep – creep
   ③ sink – sank
   ④ kneel – knelt

4. What is the right word for the blank?

   > Everyone must make these three promises in order to take part _____ the contest.

   ① in   ② of
   ③ at   ④ with

5.

> • We also hope that you will show mercy _____ the end.
> • Jessica had given a sailor Shylock's most precious ring _____ exchange for a tame monkey.

① of   ② to

③ in   ④ off

6.

> • I've set my mind _____ it, and will accept nothing else.
> • Do you mean that you have both cheated _____ us by falling in love with other men while we were away?

① on   ② at

③ to   ④ off

7. Why was Antonio worried when he went to church?

① He thought that people might say bad things about him.

② He did not know how to say the prayers.

③ He was afraid that the building might fall down.

④ He thought of the rocks that might wreck his ships.

8. What did Antonio have to give if he failed to pay back the money to Shylock?

① one of his ships

② a pound of his flesh

③ ten thousand ducats

④ gold and jewels

9. Why did Gratiano put his hands together as though he was praying?
   ① He wanted to become a priest.
   ② He wanted Antonio's ships to come back safely.
   ③ He wanted Portia to marry him.
   ④ He wanted to show Bassanio that he could behave well.

10. Why did Bassanio invite Shylock to supper?
   ① to make their deal respectable
   ② because they were great friends
   ③ to give Jessica a chance to escape
   ④ to show Launcelot what a good master he was

11. Why did Shylock say that he didn't mind Launcelot Gobbo going to work for Bassanio? Choose *two* answers.
   ① He thought that Launcelot was a lazy servant.
   ② He was tired of Launcelot being rude to him.
   ③ He thought that Launcelot would waste Bassanio's money.
   ④ He wanted Launcelot to spy on Bassanio for him.

12. What was inside the gold casket?
   ① some gold coins
   ② a few bones
   ③ a picture of a skull
   ④ nothing

13. Why didn't Portia want Bassanio to choose his casket too soon?
    ① She didn't want to marry him.
    ② She hoped that he would go away without choosing.
    ③ She wanted him to play music to her instead.
    ④ She was afraid that he would choose the wrong one and leave.

14. What was Portia's real plan while Bassanio was away?
    ① to spend her time at home, praying
    ② to go to a monastery with Nerissa
    ③ to go with Bassanio to Venice on his ship
    ④ to go secretly to Venice on the public ferry

15. Which of these reasons for showing mercy was NOT given by Portia?
    ① It blesses both the one who gives it and the one who receives it.
    ② It shows the true worth of a man.
    ③ It is required by the laws of Venice.
    ④ It is demonstrated by kings and by God.

16. Why did Antonio think it was better to die now in the courtroom?
    ① He knew that if he stayed alive, Shylock would hate him.
    ② He knew that if he stayed alive, everyone except him would be married.
    ③ He knew that if he stayed alive, everyone would think bad things about him.
    ④ He knew that if he stayed alive, he would be a very poor man.

17. What "kind and generous" thing did Antonio do for Shylock?
    ① He said he did not want his half of Shylock's money until Shylock died.
    ② He gave all his ships to Shylock.
    ③ He offered to go and search for Jessica and Lorenzo.
    ④ He gave Shylock three thousand ducats.

18. Why did Portia insist on having Bassanio's ring in the court?
    ① She regretted giving it to him and she wanted it back.
    ② She wanted to test him to see if he would keep his promise.
    ③ She forgot that she had given it to him and she liked the look of it.
    ④ She realized that it was worth nothing and wanted to give him a better one.

19. What did Bassanio plan to do the day after the court hearing?
    ① stay in Venice
    ② go back to Belmont
    ③ visit a monastery
    ④ buy a new ring

20. Where did Lorenzo think Portia had been?
    ① Venice
    ② a monastery
    ③ the court of justice
    ④ in the garden

21. Why was Nerissa upset about the ring she had given to Gratiano?
① He laughed at the words written on it.
② He said that it wasn't worth much.
③ He gave it away even though he had promised to keep it.
④ He threw it into a hole in the ground.

22. Why was Gratiano "furious" during the discussion about Bassanio's ring?
① He realized that he had been tricked.
② He discovered that Antonio had not lost his ships after all.
③ He thought that Nerissa had fallen in love with another man.
④ He found the doctor sleeping in his bed.

※ Choose the wrong part of each sentence. (23~25)

23.
He was busy to give instructions to one of his servants.
　　① 　　　② 　　　　　③ 　　④

24.
"I will be as solemn so a priest," he said.
　　① ② 　　　　③ 　　　　　④

25.

After arranging to meet at Gratiano's house in an hour time, they
     ①   ②   ③   ④

rushed away, too.

※ Choose the correct sentence. (26~27)

26. ① Our house is so miserable place.

② Our house is a miserable so place.

③ Our house is such miserable a place.

④ Our house is such a miserable place.

27. ① You are a excellent lawyer!

② What an excellent lawyer you are!

③ What you are an excellent lawyer!

④ What a excellent you are lawyer!

Memo

Memo

 Memo

Memo

Sarah J. Dodd

Sarah J. Dodd is an experienced primary school teacher who resides in the UK, but has also lived and taught in Australia. She has a PhD in Science and a certificate in Creative Writing. She has published several books for children: "An Angel Anyway" (Anyway Press, 2008) the "Little Angels" series (Lion Children's Books, 2009/10), "The Lion Picture Bible" (Lion Children's Books, 2015) and "Legs: the tale of a meerkat lost and found" (Lion Children's Books, 2015). Her poetry for children has also been highly commended and published in the anthology "Let in the Stars" (Manchester Metropolitan University, 2014).

She is currently working on further picture books for the very young, and a novel for older children.

 Smart Readers Wise & Wide **6-8**

The Merchant of Venice

Written by William Shakespeare
Retold by Sarah J. Dodd
Illustrated by Gyeonga Jeong

First Published in December 2016

Editorial Manager: Juyon Choi
Editors: Kyunghee Jang, Jiyeong Park
Designer: Eunhee Lee
Cover Designer: Eunhee Lee

Published and distributed by

 Happy House

Darakwon Bldg., 64-1 Jandari-ro, Mapo-gu, Seoul, Korea 04031
Tel: 82-2-736-2031(ext. 250)   Fax: 82-2-732-2037
Homepage: www.ihappyhouse.co.kr
Publisher: Kyudo Chung

ISBN: 978-89-6653-499-9 18740 / 978-89-6653-156-1 18740(set)

[Components]
• 1 Audio CD (Recording Studio: Aram)
• Answer Keys & Korean Translation: Free download at www.ihappyhouse.co.kr